Whispers of the
Heart

A Mosaic of Hindi and English Poetry

Alokesh Sharma

BookLeaf Publishing

India | USA | UK

Made with ❤ on the BookLeaf Publishing Platform
www.bookleafpub.in
www.bookleafpub.com

Dedication

As I turn the pages of this cherished journey, penning down the mosaic of emotions and thoughts that have found their home in "Whispers of the Heart," my heart swells with gratitude for the constellation of souls who have illuminated my path.

My revered mother, the epitome of strength and grace, your blessings and love have been my life's greatest poem. The stories you narrated, the values you instilled, and the resilience you exhibited have been the ink with which I write and the canvas upon which my words dance.

I extend my deepest gratitude to my dearest wife, the unwavering pillar of support and my companion in every heartbeat of life. Your love has been the sanctuary of peace, inspiring countless verses and breathing life into my words. Your belief in my journey has been the steadfast star guiding me through the odyssey of life and poetry.

To the cherished circle of friends, Tarun, Anil, Aman, Himan, Prabir, Bankim, Parag, Ankit and Subhraneel, the co-authors of my life's story, your camaraderie and encouragement have been the verses of joy and solace. You have been the audience to my silent whispers and the critics to my loudest thoughts, helping me refine my craft and find my voice in the symphony of words.

And to my mentors, Sunil Savara, Sajit Nair and Tarun Jain, the sculptors of my mind and spirit, I owe a debt of gratitude that words can scarcely encompass. Your wisdom has been my compass, guiding me through the intricacies of life and the nuances of poetry. You have taught me to embrace the power of words, to seek the profound in the simple, and to find the universal in the personal.

This book is a tapestry woven from the threads of love, support and inspiration each of you provides. It is a tribute to the enduring power of relationships and the transformative journey of self-discovery.

With a heart brimming with gratitude,

Alokesh Sharma.

Acknowledgement

With immense gratitude, I reflect upon the many hands and hearts that have supported me in bringing this collection to life.

To my family, whose unwavering love and encouragement have been the foundation upon which I stand, thank you. Your belief in my journey has been my guiding light.

I am also deeply grateful to my friends and mentors, whose conversations, critiques and insights have shaped both my words and my spirit. You have been my sounding boards, my critics and my champions...and for that, I am eternally thankful.

This collection is not just a reflection of my personal experiences but also of the collective influence of everyone who has walked alongside me. To all who have inspired, supported and uplifted me through this journey—this work is, in many ways, yours as much as it is mine.

With heartfelt appreciation,
Alokesh Sharma

Preface

Welcome to the pages of "Whispers of the Heart: A Mosaic of Hindi and English Poetry," a collection that has been years in the making, growing and evolving just as we do in the grand tapestry of life. This book is a sanctuary of thoughts, emotions, and reflections captured in the intimate dance of words, written in both Hindi and English. It is a journey through varied landscapes of the human experience, embracing the diversity of emotions that define our existence.

Each poem in this collection is a world of its own, born out of moments of contemplation, bursts of inspiration, and a deep-seated desire to connect with the world and with oneself. The dual language narrative adds a unique texture to this poetic odyssey, allowing the richness of Hindi and the subtlety of English to coalesce, creating a harmonious symphony of words.

The journey of compiling these poems has been as transformative as the themes they explore. As an educator and management professional, my journey has been steeped in the pursuit of understanding and facilitating human potential. This book, in many ways, is an extension of that pursuit—an exploration of the myriad ways in which we experience, perceive, and articulate our journey through life.

"Whispers of the Heart" is an invitation. An invitation to delve into the tapestry of life, to find reflections of your own experiences in these verses, and to embark on a journey of contemplation and connection. Whether you find solace in the familiar cadence of Hindi or the eloquent expressions in English, this collection is a celebration of the poetic spirit that resides within us all.

Thank you for choosing to embark on this journey with me. I hope that these pages offer you moments of reflection, connection, and inspiration.

The Uncharted Odyssey

Walking alone...
On the land untrodden,
Searching for an identity,
That hasn't yet been taken.

Who am I? Where am I heading?
I continue to search for the answer;
But is it something vague that I am seeking?
Life is something I want to conquer!

The moments have turned into a stranger.
I have lost my destination in the journey.
There is a dark cloud of dust where am a
loner.
Every second I question my destiny.

A name—is something I search for,
My existence—is what I search for,
A tale to narrate—is what I search for,
A dream to realise—is what I search for.

Tired and tethered...
I turn around to go back;
And I see a new path created,
Realising I did something that others lack.

Made footsteps for others to follow,
A new way of life that I know,
There is something in me,
And I know I'm not shallow.

Searching for identity,
I created an existence of my own.
Searching for destination,
I crafted a new journey.

I came across so far,
When with each mile I got a new avatar.
Why do I need just one name to mention?
When I have moulded so many a dimension.

I am nameless! Yes, I am!
For I refuse to get shackled by a single
identity.
Creator of a new zone I am,
For I define the new originality.

I see a new dawn on the horizon,
And I head towards it with a new vision.
Will venture into the world unseen,
Will explore into an era where no one has
been.

A never-ending journey I take,
Without any destination for enrichment's
sake.

I walk alone...
On the road,
Never taken.
I walk alone...
without an identity,
For others to reckon

I walk alone...

to places,
Never seen.

Who am I?
I am nameless,
And as nameless I have always been!

नमकीन एहसासों की बयानी

एक बेनाम सा ख्वाब देखा है...
एक बेरंग चुनरी में रंग डाला है...
एक उन्स की बूंद जीव से चखी है...
न जाने क्यों एक नमकीन सा मज़ा है।

झील में चमकती वो सूरज की आभ है...
सर्दियों में जैसे आग की तपिश है...
नदी के बहाव में वो एक ज़रूरी ठहराव है...
खत्म जो ना हो वो अनकही दास्तान है।

उसकी सांसें मेरे चेहरे पे गर्मियों की लू है...
वो पहाड़ों में गुम हो जाए वो रास्ता है...
होठों से टपकती पान की चाशनी है।

अनसोची हकीकत सामने बयान होने लगी,
नादान सी कबूतरिया मोर बन नाचने लगी।
हया के पर्दे आगोश में जल गए,
एक मीठा सा दर्द अंधेरे कोने में चुभ गए।
एक मध्यम सा शोर पहलू में गूंजने लगा,
जैसे दूर कहीं लहरें चट्टानों से टकरा गए।
जमीन पे कुरेदने का निशान बनता गया,
उसी पे चाँद के सुकून का मरहम लगते गए।
एक अंजाने जंगल में हम खोते चले गए,
तूफान में हम लहरों को रोकने चले गए।
मचलता परवाना शमा तक पहुँच ही गया,
मचलती लहरें बांध तोड़ के निकल ही गईं।

लहरों में डूबने का मज़ा भी निराला है,
एक बेरंग चुनरी मैं रंग डाला है।
रंगरेज़ बन रंगो में रंगना...
उसका नमकीन सा मज़ा है!

Dawn's Embrace

The moon finished spawning its illusion.
The morning light flaps its wings.
Stepping on to the broken dreams,
The dawn breathes.

The veil drops away.
The beams of light find their way.
Like sharp arrows tearing apart,
Weak strings of hay.

A new beginning smiles...
A new life to embrace.
A new journey to undertake...
A new air to feel.
A new dawn that breathes.

इंतज़ार का सफर

मध्यम सा लगे हर पल,
तेरे इंतज़ार में,
जैसे डूबते सूरज की चाशनी,
ढलती हुई शाम में।

थमी सी लगे हर साँस,
तेरे इंतज़ार में,
जैसे बिखरी है परछाई,
टूटे हुए आईने में।

खट्टी सी लगे हर घूँट,
तेरे इंतज़ार में,
जैसे जमी हुई काई,
रुकी हुई सी झील में।

धुंधली सी हो जाए ये नज़र,

तेरे इंतज़ार में,
जैसे जमी हुई बर्फ़ की परत,
रात के शीशे में।

आकाश में आहिस्ते से पिघलता इंद्रधनुष,
बेनाम अनामिका में लगा हुआ अंकुश...
तेरा न आना भी,
अब रुका हुआ सहर सा लगे।

तड़पती हुई तितली,
एक रेशम के जाल में,
तेरा इंतज़ार भी,
अब उसका छटपटाना सा लगे।

बुझती हुई रोशनी सी लगे यह लम्हा,
तेरे इंतज़ार में,
जैसे एक लैंटर्न रुका है,
सुबह के इंतज़ार में।

तेरा इंतज़ार लगे,
डूबते हुए सूरज की चाशनी,
ढलती हुई शाम में।

Whispers of Hope and Happiness

Some wishes just knocked,
At the window of hope.
Some aspirations just galloped,
Through the jungle of memories.
Some dreams just flew,
Over the garden of innocence.

Some beautiful moments just flew,
Past sprinkling colours of nostalgia.

Got some signs to live life,
Got some signs to live a happy life,
Got some signs to live a meaningful life.

Some smiles just touched,
The soul deep within.
Some fog just blurred,
The pains long seen.
Some light just brightened,
The lovely times that had been.

Got some signs to live life,
Got some signs to live a happy life,
Got some signs to live a meaningful life.

Some dawns just breathed,
A new-found inspiration.
Some dusk just brought,
An unseen imagination.
Some reflections just created,
An image like a beautiful hallucination.

Some beautiful moments just flew,
Past sprinkling colours of nostalgia.

Got some signs to live life,
Got some signs to live a happy life,
Got some signs to live a meaningful life.

खोज और खो जाने की कहानी

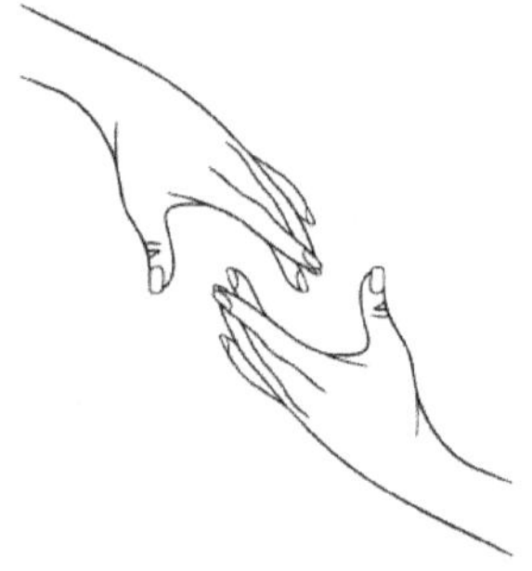

टपकती बूंद की परछाई भी,
खो जाती है पानी में उस बूंद के साथ।

बिन कहे भी बयान हो जाती है,
हाल-ए-समा इशारों के साथ।

खो जाते हैं परिंदे भी आसमान में,
अंधेरे के साथ।

मुरझा जाती है खिलखिलाती धूप भी,
शाम के ढलने के साथ।

एक मोम जलाया था,
रोशनी की उम्मीद में।
साला वो भी दगा दे गया,
पिघलने की चाह में।

हम चले तो थे,
उम्मीद की एक राह में।
वो रूह ही खत्म हो गई,
अनजानी एक खाई में।

रिवाजों को तोड़ने चला था,
एक नया लैंटर्न लेके।
वो लैंटर्न ही ज़ंग खा गया,
उन रिवाजों के बंधन में।

सुबह की धूप को,
महसूस करने चले थे।
आह...! आंखें ही चौंधिया गई,
उस धूप की चमक से।

गुम होने लगे हम भी,
क्यूँ इस भीड़ के साथ।
खो सा गया मेरा रिश्ता क्यूँ,
खुद के परछाई के साथ।

हमने तो नहीं कहा था,
कि हम अच्छे हैं,
तुम खुद ही तो कदम मिलाकर,
चल पड़े थे हमारे साथ।

नहीं मांगा था हमने,
इस धूप से छाँव।
आँचल लेकर खुद आए थे,
खो जाने के लिए हमारे साथ।

Journey of the Unseen Winds

Tethered all the way,
I see the winds sway...
Heading towards an unknown destination,
Making its journey with a thrilled
fascination...
From a hurricane to a breeze so soothing,
Always a different identity in the making...
Unknown and unseen,
Nobody knows how the journey has been...
No doubt,
Tethered all the way!
I always do see the winds sway...

धुआँ और दस्तक

धुआँ दिखा कहीं दूर मुझे...
एक मीठी सी खिलखिलाहट सी गूँजी...
नज़रों ने थोड़ी मेहनत की...
तो किसी के कंधों के उस पार...
दो नज़रें दिखीं।

थोड़ी सी छुपी हुई...
लटों के नक़ाब में...
सुट्टा सुलगा रही थी...
अपने रसीले होंठों से।

कोयले के लकीरों से...
बंधी हुई थी आँखें...
नाच रहे थे उसके कानों में...
लटकते हुए दो झुमके।

बेझिझक हंस रही थी सिर पे रखकर...
काले चश्मे का ताज...
उसके हाथों से फिसल रही थी जैसे...
सुबह की साँझ।

बैठी थी लेके वह...
नदी की अंगड़ाई...
कर रही जैसे नागिन...
डसने की तैयारी।

जल रहा था सुट्टा...
उसके नमकीन से हाथों में...
चिंगारी सुलगा रही थी...
हाय...इस दिल में।

चल पड़ी अचानक सी...
बिजली के एक झटके जैसी...
छोड़ गई एक कशिश...
लहराके अपने चुनरी से।

हम रह गए...
ताकते उस धुएं को...
दस्तक देते रह गए अपने दिल को...
बस उसकी याद में।

Hold On: A Quest for Elevation

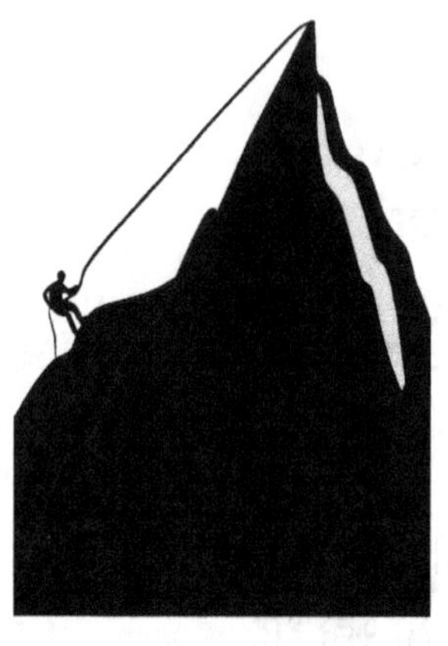

I need to climb high...
But I am stuck.
Am eager to move ahead...
But I am stuck.
How do I rise?
Somebody needs to pull me up.
I see no way...
Am all tied up.

But somehow I need to hold on...
Hold on!

Hold on, for I see light at the peak.
Hold on, for that's my only hope.
Hold on, for it's a dark vagueness below.
Hold on, for the height beckons.
Hold on, hold on, hold on...
Hold on!

I need to climb high.
Although I am stuck!!

मन की उड़ान

हौले-हौले से
एक धुन निकली है।
दिल के एक कोने से
एक चाहत निकली है।
होठों के कोने में
एक हंसी फूटी है।
आज इस पल में
एक अंजाना सा मज़ा है।

मचल के थिरक उठा
टिमटिमा के मैं जल उठा।
फड़फड़ाके अपने पंखों को
एक उड़ान में भर चला।

एक अनसुनी सी ताल बजने लगी
ये शाम जैसे सुबह में बदलने लगी।
सोंधी सी खुशबू मिट्टी से महकने लगी
तितलियां जैसे फूलों में चहकने लगी।

आसमान में मैंने इंद्रधनुष रंग दिया
रेगिस्तान में मैंने पानी छलका दिया।
तारों को मैंने धागे से पिरो दिया
सुनसान बस्ती में महफिल का शामियाना बना
दिया।

अंधेरे के आंचल से
रात को आज़ाद करने का मन है।
जलती हुई चिंगारी से
आग को रिहा करने का मन है।
पानी में टूटी सूरज की परछाई को
जोड़ने का मन किया है।

वक़्त में खो जाते
हर पल को थाम लूँगा।
खुशियों को चुराकर

ऐसे ही बाँट दूँगा।
ढोल की धमक
हर धड़कन में डाल दूँगा।

आज अंधेरे में
चमकने का मन है।
रात की धुंध को
चीरने का मन है।
तूफान की लहरों को
आज काबू में करने का मन है।

पता नहीं आज
क्या-क्या करने का मन है।
पता नहीं आज इस पल में
एक अंजाना सा मज़ा है।

In Search...

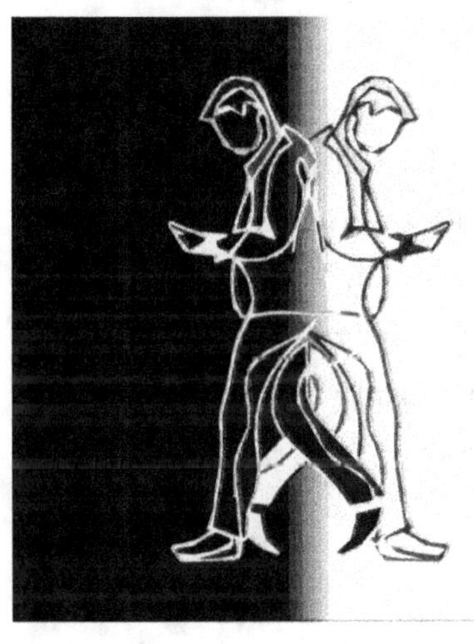

I wander around
tied and bound...
In search of
Something without which I will be well off.
I need wealth,
More than I can take in a breath...
In search of lust,
Giving love a bust...
I walk past the dust
To get what I want...
In the midst of the tiresome search

And with my mind filled with grudge...
I lose myself
And whatever I had at first...
Time slipped fast through my fingers,
like a pile of sand that never lingers...
Even though I have it in my knowledge,
I need not walk on the ledge.
Still I walk in search...
In search of things I don't need...
In search of things I won't pay a heed...
In search I walk.
I walk in search...

अंधेरों में खोई परछाई...

हमने सोचा कि कम से कम परछाई साथ देगी
ताह ज़िंदगी,
पर कमबख़्त वो भी अंधेरे में मुंह मोड़ के
चली गई।
उसके इंतज़ार में हम खुद की ही राह
तकने लगे,
चलते-चलते पन्नों पर कुछ कहानियां लिखते
चले गए।

The Echo of Serenity

A dream cloaked in the drape of night;
At the threshold of the gaze, lay a reply in
sight.

In the clamour of silence, your hint did sway;
And I wondered what did the wordless tone
convey.

The tempest that came in soon faded away;
It left some dusty memories at my soul's bay.

In the saga of withered tears, that have lost
their light;
Your unspoken words echoed with such
might.

सरगोशी में रक़्स

रात के अँधेरे में...
एक सिसक सी महसूस हुई।
साकित नसीम से गुज़र के...
माहताबी आबशार पर क़रार हुई।

नुजूम अपने सरगोशी में...
एक हसीन रक़्स को तशकील देते हुए।
जैसे तेरी नज़र में...
एक मख़फ़ी लय सी छुपी हुई।

इन दरख़्तों पर जैसे...
कोहरे का नरमी से लरज़ना।
महताब की निगरानी में...
किसी धुन पे तेरा लहराना।

ऐसा एक सुकून जहाँ...
कोई हुरूफ़ की आबादी नहीं।
बस वजूद में...
तू ही हयात की तरह बहती हुई।

The Crossroads of Our Life

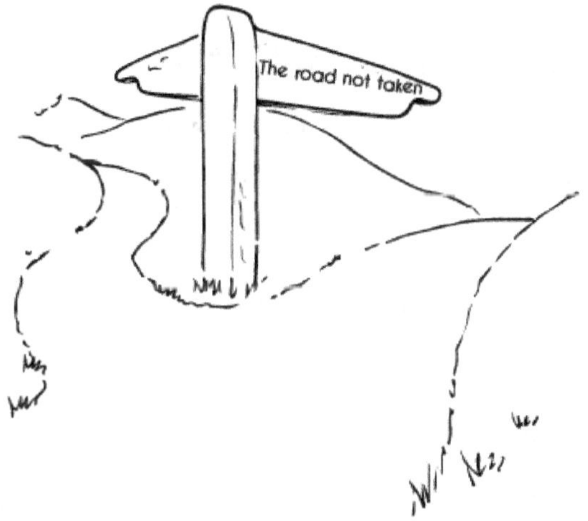

Along the road, as we walked,
We suddenly came to a standstill.
We gazed at the crossroads,
And pondered our will.

Which course felt like ours,
And which felt unknown?
The decision lies in the spirit,
For the choices are not shown.

At every turn that exists,
There is a tale to fulfil.
An attempt to grasp it,
Leaves us in wonder still.

Some turns bring grief,
Others bring bliss, to be known.
In the journey of life, each road stands on its
own.

कल की बाज़गश्त

हज़ारों गुज़रे हुए कल मेरे अक़ब में हैं।
मैं दोहरा नहीं सकता, हर लम्हे का जो नक़्श है।

ताहम मैं बे-धड़क सवेरे की तरफ़ क़दम बढ़ाता हूँ।
क्योंकि कल की बाज़गश्त की गूंज पहले ही सुन
चुका हूँ।

तज़बज़ुब की धुंध में, तवक़्क़ो ने नग़मा सुनाया।
जैसे टूटे परों के साथ परिंदा फिर से उड़ने आया।

हर ज़वाल औज का एक पैग़ाम होता है।
जिसे ये बुलंद फ़लक तहरीर करता है।

A Wait of Years

A yearning that has been...
Within me for ages.
Like a drizzle, it descended...
From the celestial stages.

The droplets...
On my lashes lingered.
And deep within my essence...
Was drenched and hindered.

Every moment of anticipation passed...
With a profound breath.
And with each gasp...
My heart dreamt anew beneath.

But when the moment arrived...
Unnoticed it drifted away.
As though the longing...
Had never been on display.

नूर की नज़ाकत

तूफ़ान की गरज से एक शमा काँपती है।
एक हस्सास नूर...
जो मजीद की तलबगार है।

उसकी लौ झपक सकती है, बुझने के क़रीब हो
सकती है।
पर फ़ज़ा की तरफ़ उठने की...
इसकी चाहत बरक़रार है।

उस हल्की सी चमक में,
एक आलम महफ़ूज़ है।
रखकर कुछ अनकहे ख़्वाब, और कुछ अनलिखी
हक़ीक़तें।

चाहे नाज़ुक हो, पर नूर क़ायम रहती है।
एक ज़ुल्मत-ज़दा भूल-भुलैया में...
बड़ी नज़ाकत से रास्ते तराशती है।

Fallen stars

In the lap of the sky,
I see the fallen stars scattered around.
Gazing at them,
Dreams are newly crowned.

But in those shattered fragments,
A hidden twinkle was found.
Maybe it was a flicker,
Of triumph in defeat unbound.

Even in the gloom of the night,

Hope could still be found.
From the fallen stars,
The radiance took its ground.

In the face of defeat,
Some victories are found.
The fallen stars,
Narrate the story profound.

वक़्त का सवाल

ख़ातिफ़ है वक़्त, या अता बख़शने वाला?
क्या यह एक दरिया रवां है, या एक लौ कांपने
वाली?
लम्हे गुज़रते हैं,
जैसे मुट्ठी में बंद धूल की तरह।
पर हर पल हमें बदलता है,
जैसे रेत बहने वाली।

आख़िर में वक़्त न तो हक़दार है,
ना ही कोई छीनने वाला।
यह बस ख़ामोशी से देखता है,
जब दुनिया अपना रूप दिखाती है।

हम तो बस राहगीर हैं
एक धार में जो न खत्म होने वाली।
इंसान तो बस महसूर है वजूद में
और बन गया मुख़्तसर ख़्वाब देखने वाला।

Rifts

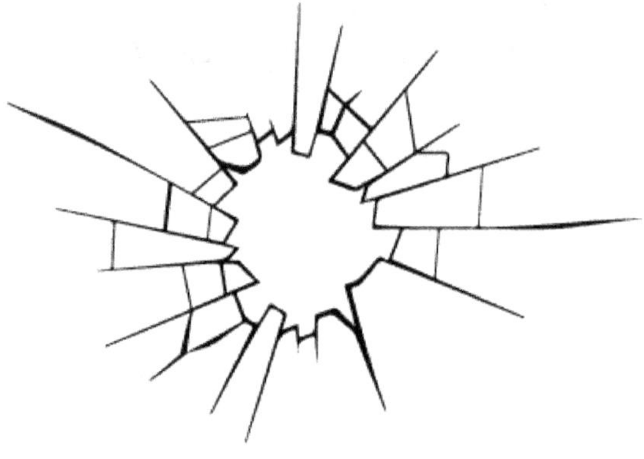

The edifices were soaring,
But the hearts had rifts.

Why do bonds among people,
Feel like distant cliffs?

Behind every laughter,
An anguish is concealed.

It didn't pour from the eyes,
But in the heart, it congealed.

The barriers we yearned,
To topple with our shifts;

We actually erected it,
But the thought was adrift.
Now mending the rifts,
Is the quest revealed.
It is wiser to mould the shape,
Of ties that were sealed.

9 789363 309852